How to Pray Out God's Perfect Will for Your Life

Rich Stocks

The following abbreviations are used for translations of the Holy Bible.

Any bold lettering or CAPITALIZATION in Scripture verses is added by the author for the purposes of emphasis only.

How to Pray Out God's Perfect Will for Your Life

ISBN for Paperback: 979-8-9851143-1-7
ISBN for eBook: 979-8-9851143-2-4

Published by Rich Stocks, Inc.
Branson, Missouri
richstocks.org

Contents

Introduction: A Personal Dedication

This book is lovingly dedicated to my mother, Birtie Gladys Stocks (February 26, 1929 – February 24, 2026)

While I was fully immersed in writing the manuscript for this book, my mother finished her journey here on Earth. She had been living with my wife and me for two and a half years and passed away peacefully in our home just two days before her 97th birthday.

My mother had not been to a doctor for many years and was taking no medications. When the time came, it took her physical body more than a week to finally let go. Watching her slowly transition from this world to the next was a very challenging experience. Because of her advanced age, I thought I was well prepared for her passing and did not expect it to be deeply emotional. But I was wrong. Many times during her final days, I had to push away from my desk and stop writing because I could not continue through the tears.

Writing about God's perfect will is one thing, but having to walk it out while saying goodbye to my mother made this message intensely real. The Scriptural principles in this book became far more than a writing project; they became my guiding light. I had to rely heavily on the very truths I am sharing with you to navigate the emotions and the decisions of this season.

I often found myself praying the exact prayers I have included in this book: "Father, show me what to do. Show me the right decisions to make and the right steps to take." I had to practice being still. I had to rely on the Holy Spirit's inward leading each day, trusting Him for every detail of her care.

My mother was a woman of quiet but consistent faith. After retiring from thirty years of hard work in a shoe factory, she didn't just settle into a rocking chair. Instead, she moved across the world to Australia for a year and later moved to Oklahoma to attend Rhema Bible College. She graduated as one of the oldest students ever to complete the program and continued to attend classes until the age of 88, proving that age does not have to be a barrier to pursuing the things of God.

Birtie Stocks was a woman of simple joys and selfless generosity. She found great contentment in walking a good distance most days to eat at her favorite fast-food restaurant, sitting in the park to read, and tending her garden. Yet, when it came to giving to others, she went all in. Christmas and birthdays were legendary; she would pile gifts so high that you literally couldn't walk through the living room after opening them all. Her heart to give extended far beyond our immediate family. Just this week, a birthday card arrived from one of her nieces—one of ten siblings. Reading that card reminded me that even on a factory worker's wages, she bought Christmas presents for that entire family.

Now that she's gone, there is so much more I wish I could tell her. If we had one last opportunity to speak, here is what I would say:

> *Mom, thank you for your godly example as both a mother and a Christian. Watching your selfless generosity through the years has taught me more about giving than words ever could. If I can become even half as generous as you were, I'll be doing well. I'm sure that so much of what you did for others went unnoticed by many of us, but looking back today, I see the great impact you had and the legacy you have left behind. You ran your race, you finished your course, and you stepped into eternity right in the center of God's perfect will. I am going to say to you the words I heard you say so many times as you talked about your grandkids over the last few years: "I miss you greatly and I love you mightily." I thank God for choosing you to be my mother, and I dedicate these pages to your honor and your memory.*

I share this deeply personal journey because I realize that many of you reading this book have gone through, or are currently going through, your own very difficult situations. We all face moments when human reasoning is inadequate, the path looks dark, and we just need to know the will of God. My prayer is that the truths in this book will give you both direction and comfort as you walk the path God has ordained for you.

Foreword by Pastor Jim Frease

God has a wonderful plan for your life, but not a wonderful life for *your plan*. Destiny is not to be *decided* but *discovered*. Just the fact that you are picking up this book tells me you have a heart to find, follow, and fulfill the will of God for your life!

In his book, *How to Pray Out God's Perfect Will for Your Life*, Rich Stocks gives you a very simple but powerful prayer from Colossians 1:9–10 that will help you do just that.

As of this writing, I have been in ministry for forty-two years, and I have prayed this simple prayer almost daily for well over three decades! I am living proof that this short prayer is truly an effective part of praying out the perfect will of God in your life!

Your destiny is determined by the words that you speak, the decisions you make, and the actions you take. This book will assist you through *monumental moments*, *pivotal points*, and *defining decisions* in your life!

You are only responsible for making the next right decision. Rich's book will assist you as you navigate the will of God for your life.

Life is not a dress rehearsal… let's make it count for Christ!

—Pastor Jim Frease
Senior Pastor of Joy Church
Mt. Juliet, Tennessee

Chapter 1: Praying Out God's Will for Your Life

Imagine unlocking God's perfect will for your life through prayer, in under a minute a day. Intrigued? Then this book is for you.

The inspiration for this work stems from a short YouTube teaching I created years ago, titled "My One-Minute Daily Prayer." That simple practice profoundly deepened my understanding of God's perfect will and how to align my life with it through prayer. I'll share this transformative prayer with you in detail later in these pages.

Our journey begins with this foundational truth from the Apostle Paul:

> *I beseech you therefore, brethren, by the mercies of God, that you present your bodies a living sacrifice, holy, acceptable to God, which is your reasonable service. And do not be conformed to this world, but be transformed by the renewing of your mind, that you may prove what is that* ***good and acceptable and perfect will of God.*** **(Romans 12:1-2 NKJV)**

I especially appreciate the Amplified Bible's rendering of the latter part of this verse:

> *...so that you may prove [for yourselves] what the will of God is, that which is good and acceptable and perfect [in* ***His plan and purpose for you****].* **(Romans 12:2 AMP)**

It's worth noting that while some translations use the word "prove," many render the word as "discern"—underscoring God's earnest desire for us to thoroughly understand His perfect will for our lives.

Another key insight into God's will comes from a specific New Testament prayer. Here is a portion of Paul's prayer for fellow believers:

> *For this reason we also, since the day we heard it, do not cease to pray for you,* **and to ask that you may be filled with the knowledge of His will in all wisdom and spiritual understanding***; that you may walk worthy of the Lord, fully pleasing Him, being fruitful in every good work and increasing in the knowledge of God;* **(Colossians 1:9-10 NKJV)**

Inspired by the Holy Spirit, Paul revealed exactly how he prayed for the saints at Colossae. He continually asked that they would be "filled with the knowledge of God's will." What a concise, impactful prayer. If you ever find yourself wondering how or what to pray, you can pray this prayer, word for word, straight from the Holy Bible. It is, without question, truly reflective of God's heart.

Why not take a moment and pray these words for yourself right now?

> "Father, fill me with the knowledge of Your will today, in all wisdom and spiritual understanding, so I can walk worthy of You, fully pleasing You, being productive in everything I do."

While I don't typically rely on feelings to discern God's will, let me ask: how did it feel to pray that short prayer just now? As I paused to pray it myself while writing, I must admit, a sense of peace came over me. This isn't about emotionalism; it's about the assurance that comes from praying God's Word. When we pray according to Scripture, we are praying according to God's perfect will.

I encourage you now to pause, note this Scripture, and commit this prayer to memory. You can pray it anytime, with absolute confidence that you are in perfect agreement with the will of God. The Lord included this verse in the Bible for us to discover and to serve as a starting point for praying out His perfect will for our lives.

Misconceptions and Misunderstandings About Prayer

Our approach to prayer is often clouded by some prevalent misconceptions and misunderstandings. These flawed ideas, often expressed by believers and even displayed on T-shirts, typically center on the mistaken belief that prayer's purpose is to somehow *twist God's arm*—to persuade Him to do something He is otherwise unwilling to do. This faulty perspective often shows up in phrases like "praying hard" or "praying long."

I wholeheartedly endorse fervency in prayer, as Jesus Himself sometimes spent entire nights communing with God. However, we are sorely mistaken if we believe we can change God's mind or coerce His response through such efforts. Rather than doing a deep dive into this subject now, suffice it to say: when you paused earlier to pray that brief prayer, you likely accomplished more in a few seconds than many achieve with a much longer prayer. My focus isn't on praying hard or long, but on praying *effectively*.

I recall hearing a well-known minister recount meeting a man who was from a group that emphasized praying at least one hour a day. This man started the conversation with, "So, how long do you pray every day?" His intent, it seemed, was to gauge the well-known minister's spirituality by how long he prayed each day. Though I have spent hours in prayer, both within a single session and over the course of a day, I have come to this realization: the greater my understanding of praying according to God's Word, the shorter and more focused my prayers have become. My primary concern is experiencing genuine fellowship with the Father in prayer and seeing tangible, effective results in every area of my life, rather than trying to impress Him or force His hand through long, repetitive prayers.

Despite my earlier intention to defer the topic of praying hard and long, this seems to be a good time to look at an important Scripture. Consider what Jesus Himself taught on this matter:

> *And when you pray, do not use* ***vain repetitions*** *as the heathen do. For* ***they think that they will be heard for their many words.*** **(Matthew 6:7 NKJV)**

This reinforces the tremendous value of the short, simple prayer we saw in the book of Colossians. It's a prayer you can pray for yourself and others every day. Each day presents new opportunities and new obstacles, and I know of no better way to embrace those opportunities and overcome the obstacles than by being filled with the knowledge of God's will. As the passage clearly indicates, Paul regularly prayed this for the saints. I am convinced this is one of the most effective prayers you could ever pray. Whenever you're unsure how to pray for yourself or someone else, pause and ask your Heavenly Father to fill them—or you—with the knowledge of His will in all wisdom and spiritual understanding.

God's Will—An Unsolvable Mystery?

It's a widespread belief that God deliberately keeps His will a mystery to us. I find it difficult to imagine living a life constantly wondering and guessing what God might want me to know or do. This misconception hinders many believers. But why does God desire for us to be filled with the knowledge of His will? Fortunately, this isn't a question we need to ponder; the answer is revealed in the Scripture we already looked at:

> *For this reason we also, since the day we heard it, do not cease to pray for you, and to ask that you may be filled with the knowledge of His will in all wisdom and spiritual understanding;* ***that you may walk worthy of the Lord, fully pleasing Him, being fruitful in every good work*** *and increasing in the knowledge of God;* **(Colossians 1:9-10 NKJV)**

Notice the explanation embedded within this verse: God wants us to be filled with the knowledge of His will so that we may "walk worthy of the Lord, fully pleasing Him, being fruitful in every good work." Simply put, God wants us to know His will so we can *do* His will and, in so doing, please Him. In fact, another Scripture reveals that this is the very purpose for which we were created:

> *Thou art worthy, O Lord, to receive glory and honour and power: for thou hast created all things, and* ***for thy pleasure they are and were created.*** **(Revelation 4:11 KJV)**

According to this divine declaration, all things, including you and me, were created for God's pleasure. Paul, inspired by the Holy Spirit, reinforces this by telling us that God desires for us to know His will so we can live in a way that brings Him joy and satisfaction.

God is not withholding His will from us. The issue often lies elsewhere: some believers may not realize that God has promised to fill them with the knowledge of His will if they ask Him in faith, expecting to receive. Or perhaps they have asked but still find themselves struggling with uncertainty. The book of James offers crucial insight into why this happens:

> *If any of you lacks wisdom, let him ask of God, who gives to all liberally and without reproach, and* ***it will be given to him. But let him ask in faith, with no doubting****, for he who doubts is like a wave of the sea driven and tossed by the wind. For* ***let not that man suppose that he will receive anything from the Lord;*** **(James 1:5-7 NKJV)**

Have you ever felt like you were being driven and tossed by the winds of life? I certainly have. During these times, do you ask God for direction? And when you ask, do you truly believe you have the answer, even before any tangible evidence appears? Several Bible translations interpret asking God for wisdom as simply asking Him "what to do." This resonates perfectly with the Colossians passage, where Paul prayed for believers to be filled with the knowledge of God's will in all wisdom and spiritual understanding.

On more than one occasion, after asking God for direction, I've found myself saying to my wife, "I just don't know what to do." And more than once, she has called me out on it. If you ask God what to do and then declare, "I just don't know what to do," it reveals a fundamental lack of belief that you *received* the wisdom you requested. The Lord's words through James are clear: if we do not ask in faith, fully convinced that we receive what we ask for, we should not expect to "receive *anything*" from Him.

These verses from James are among my favorite, go-to prayer Scriptures. Consequently, I pray this short prayer frequently—especially whenever I am faced with a new situation where I feel clueless. Here is my prayer, word for word:

> "Father, show me what to do about..."

This prayer may seem almost too basic, but the key lies in praying it in faith, believing you receive the wisdom you asked for, and then refusing to doubt that you received it until the evidence is clear. I call this concept: *Pray in Faith, Then Stay in Faith.* To receive from God, we must not only *pray* in faith but also *remain* in faith until His perfect will is fully manifested in our lives. James isn't the only place in Scripture where God invites us to pray this way. Through the prophet Jeremiah, the Lord makes this amazing promise:

> *'**Call to Me, and I will answer you,** and show you great and mighty things, which you do not know.'* **(Jeremiah 33:3 NKJV)**

Notice how closely this aligns with what we've been studying. God doesn't just tolerate our questions; He invites them. He tells us to call, He promises to answer, and He specifically says He will show us things we don't know. When we pray, "Father, show me what to do," we are responding to His invitation—expecting Him to reveal what we cannot see or figure out on our own.

Chapter 2: God's Perfect Will—What it Really Is

So, what exactly *is* the perfect will of God for your life? Can we define it in a way that is easy to understand yet all-encompassing? I believe the Lord has granted me insight into this vital question, leading to an understanding that can significantly impact your prayer life.

Here is a very concise yet comprehensive definition of God's perfect will:

1. Receiving all that God has for you to receive
2. Becoming all that God desires for you to be
3. Accomplishing all that God has called you to do

The central question then becomes: is it truly possible for you to receive all that God has for you, become all He desires, and accomplish all He has called you to do? We've already established that God wants us to be filled with the knowledge of His will, primarily so we can *do* His will and, in so doing, please Him—the very purpose for which we were created. In essence, God reveals His will so we can fulfill it. It makes no sense to ask God to fill us with the knowledge of His will if we believe His will is an unsolvable mystery.

This brings another compelling Scripture to mind, building upon our previous study in Colossians:

> *Epaphras, who is one of you, a bondservant of Christ, greets you, always laboring fervently for you in prayers,* ***that you may stand PERFECT and COMPLETE in ALL the will of God.*** **(Colossians 4:12 NKJV)**

Earlier we looked at Paul's prayer for the Colossians to continually be filled with the knowledge of God's will. Here, we find Epaphras, a member of this same church, praying a similar prayer for his fellow believers. Epaphras fervently prayed that the saints would "stand perfect and complete in all the will of God."

Consider this: why would the Lord include these verses about being filled with the knowledge of His will in the Bible if it were not possible? Notice the unmistakable emphasis of these three words in Colossians 4:12: "perfect," "complete," and "all." These words should definitively settle any lingering questions you may have about the possibility of knowing and fulfilling God's perfect will. Scripture leaves no room for doubt that God desires each of us to stand perfect and complete in all His will by receiving all that He has for us to receive, becoming all that He desires for us to be, and accomplishing all that He has called us to do.

Now, we can effectively integrate this definition of the perfect will of God into our prayers. When we want to pray for ourselves or for someone else to stand perfect and complete in all the will of God, we can pray these words with confidence:

> "Father, today help me receive all that you have for me to receive, so I can become all that you desire for me to be, so I can accomplish all that you have called me to do, so I can stand perfect and complete in all Your will."

This is not yet the full one-minute daily prayer I promised earlier, but it gets us off to a good start. When Paul noted that Epaphras was "always laboring fervently" in prayer for the saints to stand perfect and complete in God's will, it's highly unlikely he was merely repeating a short, specific phrase. Given Jesus' admonition against "vain repetitions," it's far more probable that Epaphras' fervent labor in prayer involved praying specifically about the decisions and steps that would lead them into the perfect will of God. Who knows, maybe he was praying some of the same things we are exploring in this book—that God would help them receive all, become all, and accomplish all, so they could truly stand perfect and complete in all His will.

Chapter 3:
The Priority of Receiving

I was once discussing the definition of God's perfect will with a well-known Bible teacher and friend. After sharing my three-part definition—receiving all, becoming all, and accomplishing all—he immediately responded, "What about giving all?" He evidently believed that God's will should begin with giving, rather than receiving.

This interaction reminded me of the often-overlooked priority of receiving from God. Remember, this is our starting point for fulfilling the perfect will of God. Like my friend, many Christians are convinced that giving is far more spiritual and important than receiving, and that emphasizing receiving encourages selfishness. I see this very differently when I look at the Scriptures. This misunderstanding can seriously hinder the flow of God's provision in our lives. Even though the goods are there and the Giver is willing, the connection is blocked. God hasn't changed His mind, and the supply hasn't vanished, but the pipe is clogged. And without that flow of provision, we lack the resources to take the first step on the path God has set before us. Since receiving is the first component of our definition, being unable to receive makes it impossible to move forward and fulfill God's perfect will. If my emphasis on receiving feels selfish or even rubs you the wrong way, I encourage you to keep reading. What I'm about to share will be enlightening.

My commitment is to never ask anyone to believe anything I teach without solid Scriptural support. Decades ago, the Lord revealed an acronym to me that serves as a vital safeguard: WSIT (pronounced *wiz-it*), which stands for, "What Scripture Is That?" This is one of the most important questions you can ask whenever you are presented with a teaching, a comment, or an opinion regarding the things of God. We should always measure what we hear against the only standard that matters: truth. Jesus answered the age-old question, 'What is truth?' in His prayer to the Father:

> *Sanctify them by Your truth.* ***Your word is truth.*** **(John 17:17 NKJV)**

Jesus plainly defined truth as the Word of God. I've often wondered why anyone believes they are entitled to their own opinion about something God has said. While we may interpret a Scripture differently, that is not the same as holding an opinion contrary to what God has clearly stated. Truth is truth. Each of us must sincerely ask ourselves: "What do I believe, and why do I believe it?" If you desire to stand perfect and complete in God's will, your beliefs about His will must be firmly rooted in Scripture, not sentiment or tradition. So, when my friend suggested God's will begins with giving, my immediate internal response was, "What Scripture Is That?" Though I didn't deliver the full WSIT sermon in that moment, I did proceed to share several Scriptures that had convinced me that God's will must begin with receiving. I would like to share some of those same Scriptures with you now.

Giving Your Life to Jesus?

A common phrase in Christian circles is "Give your life to Jesus." This is often used as a call for those who are not yet born again to come to the Lord. I don't see that this is Scripturally accurate when used in this context.

The Bible states that before we were born again, we were "dead in our trespasses and sins" (Ephesians 2:1, Colossians 2:13). How can anyone give their life to Jesus if they are dead in their sins? They have no life to give! The Bible tells us exactly how our Christian life begins:

> *But as many as* ***received Him****, to them He gave the right to become children of God, to those who believe in His name;* **(John 1:12 NKJV)**

Notice: your new life as a Christian did not begin with you *giving* your life to Jesus; it began the moment you *received* Jesus as your Savior and Lord. It started with Jesus *giving you* something: the right to become a child of God. Before receiving Jesus, a person has absolutely nothing to offer Him.

If that Scripture didn't fully convince you, consider this one:

For the wages of sin is death; but ***the GIFT of God is eternal life*** *through Jesus Christ our Lord.* **(Romans 6:23 KJV)**

The Bible calls eternal life a "gift." Our relationship with God doesn't begin with giving but rather with receiving Jesus and His free gift of eternal life. Scripture affirms that it is God's will for every human being to come to the saving knowledge of Jesus Christ (1 Timothy 2:4, 2 Peter 3:9). If the very first and most important step into God's will—our salvation—is based entirely on receiving, why would fulfilling the rest of His will be any different? John 1:12 establishes the foundational pattern that the perfect will of God begins with receiving. While an entire book could be written on receiving from God, let's explore a few more verses:

Come to Me, *all you who labor and are heavy laden, and* ***I will give you rest.*** **(Matthew 11:28 NKJV)**

This verse reveals *why* we come to Jesus. We don't come to give Him anything; He invites us to come and receive from Him.

Here is one of my favorite Bible verses:

Every good ***gift*** *and every perfect* ***gift*** *is from above, and comes down from the Father of lights, with whom there is no variation or shadow of turning.* **(James 1:17 NKJV)**

The key word here is "gift." A gift is simply anything that is given to you. According to this verse, all that is good and perfect in our lives is given to us by our Father God. God is the ultimate Giver; our responsibility is to receive everything He provides. The perfect will of God begins with receiving Jesus, and then continuously receiving all that God has for us. Remember our three-point definition:

1. Receiving all that God has for you to receive
2. Becoming all that God desires for you to be
3. Accomplishing all that God has called you to do

It is especially important to grasp that the very first step in fulfilling God's perfect will for your life is receiving Jesus, followed by receiving everything else God intends for you. You must receive before you can move on to steps two and three: becoming and accomplishing.

This book, however, is not merely about the will of God, but about *praying out* His perfect will. Did you know that one of the primary purposes of prayer is receiving? Consider this verse:

> *Let us therefore* **come boldly** *unto the throne of grace,* **that we may obtain** *mercy,* **and find** *grace to help in time of need.* **(Hebrews 4:16 KJV)**

According to this Scripture, we come to God in prayer to "obtain" and "find." In other words, we come to *receive.* If you fail to understand this truth, or if you mistakenly believe that focusing on receiving indicates selfishness, you will lack the boldness this verse identifies as essential for obtaining what you desire from God. As we discussed earlier, when we ask God for something in prayer, we must do so in faith and without doubt, knowing that doubt will prevent us from receiving *anything* from Him.

Receiving Power from on High

You are likely familiar with what many call the Great Commission—the monumental assignment Jesus gave His disciples before He ascended to Heaven. It's recorded in all four Gospel accounts (Matthew 28:18-20, Mark 16:15-16, Luke 24:46-49, John 20:21), with Mark's account stating:

> *And He said to them, 'Go into all the world and preach the gospel to every creature.'* **(Mark 16:15 NKJV)**

The fact that these were Jesus' final words before leaving Earth underscores just how important they are. This was His farewell charge. While often emphasized from pulpits as a cornerstone of Christian service, the Great Commission represents the *accomplishing all that God has called you to do* component of His perfect will. It is indeed something God has instructed us to do.

But I want to draw your attention to a critical instruction Jesus gave His disciples *before* they were to launch on this global mission. This was a prerequisite, essential to accomplishing what God had called them to do:

> *And being assembled together with them,* ***He commanded them not to depart from Jerusalem, but to wait for the Promise of the Father,*** *'which,' He said, 'you have heard from Me; for John truly baptized with water, but you shall be baptized with the Holy Spirit not many days from now.'...* ***But ye shall receive power, after that the Holy Ghost is come upon you: and ye shall be witnesses unto me*** *both in Jerusalem, and in all Judaea, and in Samaria, and unto the uttermost part of the earth.* **(Acts 1:4-5, 1:8 NKJV/KJV)**

This passage perfectly outlines the divine order, confirming the three components of God's perfect will:

1. Receiving all that God has for you to receive: They were to wait for and *receive* "the Promise of the Father," the Holy Spirit.
2. Becoming all that God desires for you to be: Upon receiving power, they would *become* effective witnesses.
3. Accomplishing all that God has called you to do: Only then were they equipped to go into all the world and *accomplish* their divine calling.

Before they could *accomplish* their mission, they first had to *receive* something—power from on high—so they could *become* effective witnesses. Much of the emphasis in the church has been on the *going and preaching* rather than first prioritizing the *receiving and becoming.* This pattern isn't limited to global evangelism; it's often present in the personal lives of many believers. Before receiving this revelation, I often found myself praying, "Lord, what do you want me to do?" While I still pray that prayer, I now include the necessary preceding elements, making it far more effective:

> "Father, today help me receive all that You have for me to receive, so I can become all that You desire for me to be, so I can accomplish all that You have called me to do."

If you've been asking God for direction but find yourself lacking clear guidance, perhaps there is something you need to *receive* and *become* first, before you can go and *do*.

Receiving Before Giving

The principle of receiving extends into every area of life, including our spiritual, physical, and financial well-being. For decades, I taught on material giving and receiving, often echoing the common sentiment that one must give before they can expect to receive. This is frequently framed as "sowing and reaping" or "seedtime and harvest." It sounds logical: we must sow before we can reap, right?

I, too, believed this until the Lord helped me see the truth I'm sharing in this book. If you believe sowing must precede reaping, have you ever asked yourself: "Where does the seed come from?" How can you sow anything if you don't first receive the seed? Here is a key Scripture that sheds more light on this truth:

But this I say: He who sows sparingly will also reap sparingly, and he who sows bountifully will also reap bountifully. So let each one give as he purposes in his heart, not grudgingly or of necessity; for God loves a cheerful giver. And God is able to make all grace abound toward you, that you, always having all sufficiency in all things, may have an abundance for every good work. As it is written: 'He has dispersed abroad, He has given to the poor; His righteousness endures forever.' ***Now may He who supplies seed to the sower,*** *and bread for food, supply and multiply the seed you have sown and increase the fruits of your righteousness,* **(2 Corinthians 9:6-10 NKJV)**

This passage is a cornerstone for understanding giving. While the first part emphasizes the relationship between sowing and reaping, the latter verses reveal a critical truth: *before* we can sow, God must first supply the seed. No one can give anything without first receiving something to give, and no one can sow seed without first receiving that seed. In other words, the entire law of sowing and reaping does not originate with *our* actions; it begins with God and with us first receiving from Him. This connects back to the truth we discussed regarding "giving your life to Jesus"—we have nothing to give until we first receive from God.

What I appreciate most about this teaching is how it leaves no room for pride. If we have been bountiful sowers and have reaped abundantly, leading to great prosperity, we must be mindful to give God all the glory. Our prosperity doesn't begin with our sowing; it begins with God giving us seed to sow.

More Blessed to Give Than to Receive

I want to make sure my emphasis on receiving is not interpreted as diminishing the importance of giving. Jesus taught giving, Paul taught giving, and I strongly believe in, teach, and practice giving. We even see the saints at Corinth being commended for giving out of their "deep poverty" (2 Corinthians 8:1-5). We see Jesus observing a poor widow who gave all she had and using this as a teaching example for His disciples. (Mark 12:41-44). Our Father God is the ultimate Giver and, as His children, we have His giving nature. Here is a well-known Scripture to remember:

> *And remember the words of the Lord Jesus, that He said, 'It is* **more blessed to give** *than to receive.'* **(Acts 20:35 NKJV)**

Two words stand out to me as I read this verse. These are the words *more blessed.* If you were in a restaurant and your server asked you if you wanted *more* coffee, what does this imply? The only way for you to receive more coffee is if you already have or have already had some. This is my point in teaching that the will of God *must* begin with receiving. Before I can *become* the giver that God wants me to *be*, and *accomplish* all that He wants me to *do* through my giving, I must *receive* all that He has for me to receive.

The verse we just looked at tells us that receiving is a blessing but that giving is an even greater blessing. Why? I see a two-fold answer. First, receiving is a blessing to you, but the blessing of giving extends beyond you and includes all those you give to. Second, we have already seen that God refers to our giving as sowing seed, and we are told that He will multiply the seed we sow (2 Corinthians 9:6-10). This means that when you give, God's plan is that you always get back *more* than you gave. Jesus taught this principle in the following verse:

> *Give, and* ***it will be given to you: good measure, pressed down, shaken together, and running over*** *will be put into your bosom. For with the same measure that you use, it will be measured back to you.* **(Luke 6:38 NKJV)**

Yes, God emphasizes giving throughout the Bible, but He also emphasizes receiving. Many of the Scriptures that talk about giving make it clear that, as you give, God intends for you to *receive even more.* So while giving is the greater blessing for the reasons I have mentioned, I stand my ground on the fact that this does not mean that giving is *more important* than receiving.

Also, I want to make clear that I am not teaching against "Giving your life to the Lord." In fact, this exact phrase is used in 2 Corinthians 8:5. But this only applies to those who have received Jesus.

Chapter 4: Divine Positioning: Place, People, Activities, and Timing

As we continue to build our understanding of praying out God's perfect will, it's time to add another layer to our daily prayer. We've established the pattern: asking the Lord to help us receive all He has for us, so we can become all He desires, so we can accomplish all He has called us to do. However, there are specific conditions that must be met to make this a reality in your life.

Many years ago, while ministering, I was prompted to make a bold statement: anyone who grasped the message I was about to share would never forget it. My teaching focused on the importance of being in the right places, with the right people, doing the right activities, at the right time.

I call these the prerequisites to receiving from God. Consider this: how can we possibly receive all, become all, and accomplish all if we are not strategically positioned in the right place? Several Scriptural examples come to mind.

Recall that after Jesus gave the Great Commission, He instructed His disciples to "wait in Jerusalem until they be endued with power from on high" (Acts 1:4). Where was this power to be sent? To an upper room in Jerusalem. Before they could receive what God had for them, they had to be in the right place where the promised power would be poured out. God's instructions often contain critical details that determine whether you receive His provision.

Consider the healing of the blind man in John chapter 9. Jesus made mud, applied it to the man's eyes, and then commanded him, "Go, wash in the Pool of Siloam." For the man to receive his healing, he had to be in the right place: the Pool of Siloam. Receiving all that God has for you often requires being exactly where He wants you to be.

A Place Called "There"

One of the most striking illustrations of divine positioning can be seen in the life of Elijah:

> *And Elijah the Tishbite, of the inhabitants of Gilead, said to Ahab, "As the Lord God of Israel lives, before whom I stand, there shall not be dew nor rain these years, except at my word." Then the word of the Lord came to him, saying, "Get away from here and turn eastward, and hide by the Brook Cherith, which flows into the Jordan. And it will be that you shall drink from the brook, and* ***I have commanded the ravens to feed you THERE.****" So he went and did according to the word of the Lord, for he went and stayed by the Brook Cherith, which flows into the Jordan. The ravens brought him bread and meat in the morning, and bread and meat in the evening; and he drank from the brook.* **(1 Kings 17:1-6 NKJV)**

Elijah, having prophesied a severe drought, was now subject to the very famine he foretold. Yet it was never God's will for His prophet to starve. God had a supernatural plan for provision, but for Elijah to receive that provision, he had to cooperate by being in the *right place*. God's instructions were remarkably precise: the Brook Cherith. What if Elijah, on his way, had seen another seemingly sufficient brook? He might have rationalized, "It probably doesn't matter which brook, as long as there's water." But the detail was crucial: "I have commanded the ravens to feed you *there*." "There" was the Brook Cherith, and nowhere else.

The story continues:

> *And it happened after a while that the brook dried up, because there had been no rain in the land. Then the word of the LORD came to him, saying, 'Arise, go to Zarephath, which belongs to Sidon, and dwell* ***there****. See, I have commanded a widow* ***there*** *to provide for you.'* **(1 Kings 17:7-9 NKJV)**

The repetition of "there" is significant. God specifically directed Elijah to Zarephath, where a certain poor widow had already been commanded to take care of him. Are you beginning to grasp the magnitude of being in the right place to receive all that God has for you? How often have we missed God's perfect will because our human reasoning suggested a different, more convenient, or more attractive alternative? There is no indication that if Elijah had gone somewhere else, he would have experienced the same miraculous outcome. God had a plan and a person, but it all hinged on Elijah being in the right place.

It's worth noting that God did not reveal all the steps to Elijah ahead of time; He led him one step at a time. When Elijah was sent to the brook, he might have assumed he would stay there until the famine was over. He was probably surprised, and perhaps even questioned God, when the brook began to dry up: "God, did I miss something? Now what?" While we don't know for sure what Elijah's thought process was, I have found questioning and second-guessing the will of God to be common among fellow believers. There is no indication that Elijah's daily leading came through a spectacular prophetic anointing. It is far more likely that he had to navigate life one step at a time just like we do. I am confident Elijah was praying earnestly for his next instruction as the brook dwindled before his eyes.

Here is some amazing news: as a Christian believer, you possess an ability that Elijah didn't have. We see this confirmed in the following Scripture:

> *For as many as are* ***led by the Spirit of God****, these are sons of God.* **(Romans 8:14 KJV)**

As a child of God, you are capable of being led by the Spirit of God. You can be filled with the knowledge of God's perfect will, enabling you to make the right decisions regarding the right places, the right people, the right activities, and the right timing. This Spirit-led guidance is essential for receiving all that God has for you.

Supernatural, Not Spectacular

Following the leading of the Spirit of God is, by its very nature, a supernatural experience. The word *supernatural* simply means "not attributable to natural forces." However, I've observed many believers who confuse the supernatural with the spectacular, expecting God to lead them in dramatic, earth-shaking ways.

My experience has taught me that, most often, when facing a major decision, the answer comes as a still, small knowing on the inside. One moment I might be entirely unsure of the next step, and suddenly a clear path emerges with an overwhelming sense of peace and conviction. This inward leading is often subtle, and learning to be sensitive to it may take time to develop. Remember, as we discussed earlier from the book of James, once we ask God for wisdom concerning a matter, we are to believe we received it *when we prayed* and then refuse to doubt as time passes. Know this: it is time, not God, that is the great tester of our faith. If every prayer of faith brought an immediate, *visible* answer, faith's role in our lives would be minimal. However, as time passes, doubt will attempt to convince us that God neither heard nor answered our prayer. This is where faith becomes our anchor.

Walk by Faith or Get Fleeced

Are you familiar with the Old Testament account of Gideon's fleece? Gideon, despite a divine commission and a prior angelic visitation, sought physical confirmation of God's will to defeat the Midianites. Let's briefly review the account found in Judges 6:

- **Divine Commission:** God called Gideon to lead Israel against their oppressors.
- **Gideon's Doubt:** Gideon was hesitant, needing reassurance of victory.
- **The First Test:** Gideon requested dew on a wool fleece, but dry ground around it. God complied.
- **The Second Test:** Still uncertain, he then asked for the opposite: a dry fleece and wet ground. Once again, God granted his request.
- **Final Confirmation:** These signs finally convinced Gideon that God was with him.

While God graciously indulged Gideon, praying for God to reveal or confirm His will with a physical sign—a "fleece"—is not Scriptural for us as New Testament saints. We have already seen that as the children of God, we are to be led by the Holy Spirit within us, not by external signs or circumstances. One of the most common yet concerning prayers I've heard through the years is, "Lord, if it's Your will, open the door; if it's not Your will, close the door." When a person prays this prayer, they are asking God to lead them in a manner contrary to how He instructs us to live and walk. As the Holy Spirit declares through the Apostle Paul:

> *For we walk by faith,* ***not by sight*****:** **(2 Corinthians 5:7 KJV)**

Let me reiterate: if you ask God to lead you by external signs or circumstances, such as open or closed doors, you are asking Him to lead you in a way that is contrary to walking by faith.

Even the early apostles made a similar error shortly after Jesus' resurrection. You can read about this in Acts 1:15-26, which describes how they went about choosing a replacement for Judas:

- **The Need:** Peter declared a need to replace Judas in the apostleship.
- **The Candidates:** Two men were nominated: Joseph (Barsabbas) and Matthias.
- **The Prayer:** The apostles prayed, asking God to show which of the two He had chosen.
- **Casting Lots:** They "cast lots" (a method of chance, like drawing straws) to discern God's will, believing it would reveal His choice.
- **The Result:** The lot fell to Matthias, and he was added to the eleven.

Jesus had told the original twelve apostles they would sit on twelve thrones judging the twelve tribes of Israel (Matthew 19:28, Luke 22:30). Judas Iscariot forfeited his right to one of these thrones (Acts 1:20). However, we find no indication that God instructed them to find a replacement for Judas, nor do we see evidence that their method is Scriptural. They were not endeavoring to be led by the Spirit of God or to walk by faith; instead, they put out a fleece akin to Gideon's actions in the Old Testament, asking God to confirm His will through a physical sign.

The Bible does not mention Matthias again. We have no reason to believe that he was God's choice to sit on one of those twelve thrones. It is my personal belief that the Apostle Paul was God's chosen replacement for Judas, an apostle hand-picked by Jesus Himself, whose ministry and letters continue to shape the church today. Think about it: the eleven apostles "cast lots," today's equivalent of rolling dice or drawing straws, to determine who would sit on one of twelve thrones throughout all eternity. They were not being led by the Spirit of God. Yes, they prayed, but instead of waiting for direction from within before moving forward, they looked for an outward sign. The shift from seeking outward signs to relying on the inward leading of the Holy Spirit marks a defining distinction for the believer today.

The Right People

Let's pause to reinforce our understanding. We've established that God's perfect will for your life can be summarized in three components:

1. Receiving all that God has for you to receive
2. Becoming all that God desires for you to be
3. Accomplishing all that God has called you to do

The sequential order of these components is non-negotiable: we must receive before we become, and become before we can accomplish. Additionally, we've identified prerequisites essential to effectively receiving God's blessings: being in the right places, with the right people, engaging in the right activities, at the right time.

I am convinced that how we prioritize these prerequisites also matters. God chose a poor widow to sustain Elijah during the famine, making her one of the *right people* in his life for fulfilling God's plan. Yet Elijah would never have found the right person if he hadn't first found the right *place.* The right people, integral to fulfilling God's will, are out there. The question is, "Where?" You are far more likely to encounter the right people when you position yourself in the right place.

Consider the fascinating story of Cornelius:

> *There was a certain man in Caesarea called Cornelius, a centurion of what was called the Italian Regiment, a devout man and one who feared God with all his household, who gave alms generously to the people, and prayed to God always. About the ninth hour of the day he saw clearly in a vision an angel of God coming in and saying to him, "Cornelius!" And when he observed him, he was afraid, and said, "What is it, lord?" So he said to him, "Your prayers and your alms have come up for a memorial before God. Now send men to Joppa, and send for Simon whose surname is Peter. He is lodging with Simon, a tanner, whose house is by the sea. He will tell you what you must do."* **(Acts 10:1-6 NKJV)**

Though Cornelius feared God, he was not born again since he had not yet heard the gospel message. God, in His earnest desire for Cornelius and his household to know Jesus, sent an angel with very specific instructions. The angel's concluding words are particularly significant: "He will tell you what you must do." This aligns perfectly with our understanding of God's perfect will. Before Cornelius could receive Jesus and embark on God's plan for his life, he had to find the right place to meet the right person who would then tell him what to do. Notice the remarkable precision of God's instructions. The right place for Cornelius was not just the city of Joppa; God essentially gave him the exact house number where he would find Simon Peter. As you continue reading Acts chapter 10, you'll witness how being in the right places, with the right people, performing the right activities, at the right time, led to Cornelius and his entire household hearing the gospel and receiving salvation.

The Right Activities

Finding the right place and connecting with the right people are essential, but this may not always be enough. Sometimes, taking additional steps of action will be necessary to fulfill the will of God.

In the first chapter of James, we learned that when we lack wisdom, we can simply ask God and He will show us what to do. That's why this has become one of my favorite and most frequent prayers:

> "Father, show me what to do."

It may sound too simple, but I am thoroughly convinced this is the most effective way to ask God for wisdom. Wisdom, at its core, is knowing what God wants you to do, and then doing it.

Here is a personal example that vividly illustrates just how effective this type of prayer can be. One morning, while walking my dog, I experienced excruciating pain in my foot. It was so severe that walking became a struggle. When we moved into our current neighborhood, one of the first people to introduce herself made it clear that she and her husband were “staunch Baptists”—a phrase that has, over the years, become a point of playful humor between us. But on that particular painful morning, the last thing I, a faith and healing preacher, wanted was for my staunch Baptist neighbors to see me hobbling down the street. So I prayed these exact words:

> "Father, I know what You’ve done about my health and healing, but what do You want *me* to do about this pain in my foot?"

The answer came immediately—not as an audible voice, but as a distinct internal knowing, as clear as if someone were speaking inside me: "Go home, get that pair of shoes out of the closet that you stopped wearing, and wear them around the house for a couple of days."

You might be thinking, "That sounds crazy!" Indeed, it did. But guess what? It worked! As soon as the thought about the shoes entered my mind, I knew it wasn't my own idea but God giving me the wisdom I had asked for. It wasn't time to pray, to read healing Scriptures, or to make faith declarations. It was time to exercise my faith by *doing* exactly what God had instructed me to do. I was so excited that I hobbled as fast as I could to get home and put on those shoes. Within a couple of days, all the pain in my foot was gone.

Now, if pain ever strikes my foot again, will I automatically reach for that same pair of shoes? No. It doesn't work that way. The Lord wasn't revealing a pair of *magic* shoes; ironically, I had stopped wearing them because they seemed to *cause* discomfort. This experience taught me that God may sometimes lead us to do something that defies human reason and may even appear foolish, but is actually a manifestation of His wisdom. The following Scriptures come to mind:

> *But* ***God hath chosen the foolish things of the world to confound the wise;*** *and God hath chosen the weak things of the world to confound the things which are mighty;* **(1 Corinthians 1:27 KJV)**

> *Because* ***the foolishness of God is wiser than men;*** *and the weakness of God is stronger than men.* **(1 Corinthians 1:25 KJV)**

Please don't interpret this as a license to get weird and start looking for foolish things to do. You may never be led to do something this illogical in your lifetime, and if you are, it will likely be the exception, not the rule. Nevertheless, remaining open to God's instructions, no matter how unusual they seem, is vital.

Consider another classic Biblical example:

> *So it was, as the multitude pressed about Him to hear the word of God, that He stood by the Lake of Gennesaret, and saw two boats standing by the lake; but the fishermen had gone from them and were washing their nets. Then He got into one of the boats, which was Simon's, and asked him to put out a little from the land. And He sat down and taught the multitudes from the boat. When He had stopped speaking, He said to Simon, "Launch out into the deep and let down your nets for a catch." But Simon answered and said to Him, "Master, we have toiled all night and caught nothing; nevertheless at Your word I will let down the net." And when they had done this, they caught a great number of fish, and their net was breaking. So they signaled to their partners in the other boat to come and help them. And they came and filled both the boats, so that they began to sink.* **(Luke 5:1-7 NKJV)**

Many believers read about the miraculous works in the Bible but fail to consider that God's answer to their prayers may be manifested in a similar fashion. There will be times when God leads you to release your faith through an action that, to human reasoning, appears foolish. Peter and his companions were seasoned fishermen; Jesus was just a carpenter turned preacher. Peter might have thought, "Seriously? I'm the expert fisherman here. What could *You* possibly teach *me* about fishing?" Furthermore, my understanding is that their usual method was shallow-water fishing, yet Jesus commanded them to "launch out into the deep." They had toiled all night, following their professional judgment, and caught nothing. Now, Jesus was asking them to do something unconventional, something no experienced fisherman would even consider, and the result was a net-breaking, boat-sinking load of fish!

Peter, though likely still processing Jesus' true identity, expressed his reluctance but ultimately obeyed: "nevertheless at Your word I will let down the net." Even though Peter was in the right place, with the right people, at the right time, he could have disregarded Jesus' instruction and gone home empty-handed. If you are facing a situation right now that seems resistant to your prayers and efforts, I strongly recommend praying this simple prayer right now:

> "Father, show me what to do."

Narrowing Your Focus

When I pray about being in the right places for God's perfect will in my life, I start broadly and then narrow my focus: Am I in the right country? The right state? The right city? The right neighborhood? The right house? We saw how important the details were with Cornelius.

This approach is especially important when it comes to your employment. Many people spend a significant portion of their lives at work—often forty hours or more each week for decades. How significant is it, then, to ensure you are in the right place when it comes to your career? Far too often, I see individuals making employment decisions based solely on salary, benefits, and perks, neglecting to seek God's perfect will for the *place* where they may invest so many years of their lives. Whether you are deciding on a career, a city, a relationship, or just the next step in this season of your life, intentionally positioning yourself is a fundamental key to receiving all He has for you.

Chapter 5:
A Book Written About You

What if I told you that before you were even born, God wrote a book about you, recording His perfect will for each day of your life? Have a look at this stunning truth:

> *You saw me before I was born and* ***scheduled each day of my life before*** *I began to breathe.* ***Every day was recorded in your book!*** **(Psalm 139:16 TLB)**

Wow! This verse reveals something extraordinary: God foresaw every single day of your life, planned each one, and recorded them in a book before you ever drew your first breath. Evidently, this *book* represents God's master plan for your life—His perfect will laid out from beginning to end. To me, this stands out as one of the most remarkable Scriptures in the entire Bible. I'm convinced that this divine foresight speaks directly to the "good, acceptable, perfect will of God" for your life, referenced in Romans 12:2.

I have a minister friend who has experienced many profound visitations with the Lord throughout his decades of ministry. I vividly recall being in one of his services when he was *caught up* in such an encounter. He had a habit of pacing back and forth across the front of the auditorium as he taught God's Word. Suddenly, he froze. He stood absolutely still. I initially thought he had stopped to capture a divine thought. Five minutes passed, then ten, then thirty. The next thing I knew, an hour and a half had passed, and he was still frozen like a statue. If he hadn't been standing, we would have thought he was dead. It was a Wednesday night service, and he had already been teaching for a considerable time. Since it was a school night, I decided to take my three young children home and put them to bed after ninety minutes of silence. That night was a captivating and unforgettable experience, and I am forever thankful the Lord allowed me to witness it.

The following Sunday morning, the minister shared with the church the details of his encounter. He explained that as he closed his eyes, he saw a stairway, which he ascended until he met Jesus. Jesus then escorted him to what he described as a vast library, filled with books stretching as far as the eye could see. Jesus took a book from a shelf and said, "This is the book of your life." He directed the minister's attention to Psalm 139:16, explaining, "As you were being formed in your mother's womb, the Lord God wrote this book from start to finish." As my friend gently thumbed through the pages, he noticed something striking: there were blank pages. He questioned Jesus about these, and Jesus explained, "These represent periods of time when you missed the perfect will of God. By the grace of God, and because of My cleansing blood, these missed days are not being held against you." Perhaps we should all pause here, exhale a sigh of relief, and say, "Thank You."

My friend was surprised, discovering more blank pages than he had anticipated. He confessed to Jesus that ever since he accepted the call to ministry, he had diligently sought to follow God's perfect will. He genuinely questioned how there could possibly be so many blank pages in his book. It was at this point that the story became even more intriguing. Jesus further explained, "To fulfill God's will for your life, it sometimes requires other people to also fulfill God's will for theirs." Even as I write this, the realization that my ability to fulfill God's will is linked to others is sobering. It gives me what I call *Heavenly vibes*—my term for spiritual goosebumps. Think about this for a moment. I've been emphasizing the significance of right places, right people, right activities, and right timing. Yet, until I heard the details of this visitation, I had never fully grasped that my ability to fulfill God's will might be directly dependent upon another person fulfilling God's will for *their* life. In essence, we are all intricately connected, intertwined, and networked together within the Body of Christ. This matches perfectly with the Biblical description of the Body of Christ as one body with many members, each having a unique function (1 Corinthians 12:12-27, Romans 12:4-5).

Let's examine a portion of these passages:

> *But now indeed there are many members, yet one body. And the eye cannot say to the hand, 'I have no need of you'; nor again the head to the feet, 'I have no need of you.' No, much rather, those members of the body which seem to be weaker are necessary. And* ***if one member suffers, all the members suffer with it****; or if one member is honored,*

all the members rejoice with it. **(1 Corinthians 12:20-22, 26 NKJV)**

A few things stand out here. Each individual member of your physical body is dependent upon all other members, and each member can only fulfill its function if the others are fulfilling theirs. This makes it clear that your ability to fulfill God's perfect will isn't solely dependent on you. There will undoubtedly be aspects of God's will that you cannot achieve if others, whom God intended to be connected to you, are operating outside of His will. Moreover, if one member suffers, *all* suffer with it.

In the visitation, Jesus explained this interconnectedness as the reason for many of the blank pages in the minister's book. Even though he was doing everything he knew to do to fulfill God's will, there were times he simply couldn't because others, who were essential to that perfect will, were not in the right places, with the right people, doing the right activities, at the right time. Aren't you thankful for God's mercy? When we are unable to fulfill God's perfect will because of the choices others have made, He provides a blank page rather than marking it as a failure. You might be thinking this doesn't apply to you because you don't perceive your calling as a big deal to God or anyone else. However, we just read that even the "weaker" members are necessary. If you are a Christian, you are a member of the Body of Christ, and your function is essential to God's plan for all of us. This makes learning to pray out the perfect will of God all the more important for you. No member can say to another, "I don't need you," and consequently, none of us can say, "I'm not needed." This truth should help you grasp just how important your role is in God's great plan for His church.

As my friend's visitation continued, Jesus shared another example to emphasize just how connected we all are in fulfilling God's will. He used the example of Paul and Barnabas:

> *Now in the church that was at Antioch there were certain prophets and teachers: Barnabas, Simeon who was called Niger, Lucius of Cyrene, Manaen who had been brought up with Herod the tetrarch, and Saul. As they ministered to the Lord and fasted, the Holy Spirit said, 'Now* ***separate to Me Barnabas and Saul for the work to which I have called THEM.****' Then, having fasted and prayed, and laid hands on them, they sent them away.* **(Acts 13:1-4 NKJV)**

Later in Acts chapter 13, Saul is referred to as Paul, so I will refer to this ministry pair as Paul and Barnabas. My research indicates they worked together for at least 15 years. But then, an unfortunate event occurred that led to the dissolution of their partnership:

> *Then after some days Paul said to Barnabas, 'Let us now go back and visit our brethren in every city where we have preached the word of the Lord, and see how they are doing.' Now Barnabas was determined to take with them John called Mark. But Paul insisted that they should not take with them the one who had departed from them in*

Pamphylia, and had not gone with them to the work. Then ***the contention became so sharp that they parted from one another.*** *And so Barnabas took Mark and sailed to Cyprus; but Paul chose Silas and departed, being commended by the brethren to the grace of God. And he went through Syria and Cilicia, strengthening the churches.* **(Acts 15:36-41 NKJV)**

God's perfect will for Paul and Barnabas was that they work together as a team. The only way either of them could fulfill God's original plan in that context was if the other did as well. When this disagreement arose, the moment one decided they were done working with the other, God's perfect will for that partnership was affected. Did this mean God was finished with both of them? Absolutely not! The text shows Paul chose Silas, and they traveled throughout the region, ministering to believers and strengthening the churches. It is safe to assume the Lord continued ministering through Barnabas also. God did not revoke His call upon their lives even though they deviated from His original plan. This is encouraging news for you and me. If the man who penned most of the New Testament could miss it in a crucial relationship, and yet God continued to work with him, there is certainly hope for us.

Jesus used this example to explain to my friend why there were blank pages in his book, even when there seemed to be no logical explanation. "Many of these blank pages do not signify that you personally missed God's will, but rather that the plan involved connections with other people."

Here's where the story gets even better, revealing the immeasurable depth of God's grace. Jesus further explained that even though God records His perfect will in a book for every human before birth, when a Christian believer deviates from the path that leads to the fulfillment of that perfect will, there is grace. Not only does God not hold this against us, but He actually begins rewriting the book. Jesus shared that the blank pages represented times when God *rewrote the plan.*

Jesus used the example of Paul and Barnabas to illustrate this rewriting process. God's perfect will was for them to work together as a team, which they did for many years. But they eventually parted ways, and while some may argue this was God's will, consider the context. They ceased working together due to "sharp contention"—a disagreement that escalated into a hostile argument. The Holy Spirit had specifically separated them "for the work," implying a divine partnership. If that plan were to change, surely it would be the Holy Spirit Who communicated the change, not an unfavorable circumstance or human strife. I've already touched on the dangers of trying to interpret God's will through circumstances. As we saw, God did not change His mind about either Paul or Barnabas being called to ministry, even though His *perfect* will for their partnership was affected. I strongly suspect that if we could see the books of Paul's and Barnabas' lives, we would find blank pages where their separation occurred, representing God's compassionate rewriting of their individual paths.

Chapter 6: God's GPS—The Path and the Master Plan

The letters GPS, or Global Positioning System, refer to the satellite-based radio-navigation system commonly used for driving directions. It is standard in nearly every modern smartphone and automobile, providing real-time directions to our destinations. I want to introduce you to a new version of GPS: *God's Positioning System.*

Before I elaborate, let me share a personal experience that opened my understanding to this analogy and its profound connection to God's perfect will. I was in my hotel room in Broken Arrow, Oklahoma, the night before a Bible teaching engagement. As is my practice, I had spent considerable time in preparation—not just preparing the message but preparing *myself.* I was following the wisdom of a well-known minister who once observed that he spent more time preparing *the man* (referring to himself) than he did his messages. I had been sitting for hours, and as I stood to walk to the restroom, these words came up inside me: "At this moment, you are in the center of My perfect will."

This caught me completely off guard, shaking me to my core, but I knew with absolute certainty that the Lord had spoken to me. My immediate thought was one of skepticism: I couldn't possibly be in the center of God's perfect will. I knew for sure that there were several projects I was behind on, including several books I had not even started.

But this was one of those undeniable experiences where you know that you know that you know that God is unveiling something life-changing. Before I could even verbalize my questions, a clear image flashed into my mind—not a vision, but a natural example designed to illustrate a spiritual truth. I understood that in the big picture, God's long-term plan, I had indeed stalled or strayed at times, attempting to accomplish His will through human reasoning rather than Spirit-led guidance.

But then I realized the emphasis on these particular words: "At this moment." Suddenly, the GPS analogy became crystal clear. Imagine planning a road trip from New York to Los Angeles. You input your destination, and your GPS plots the route. The GPS has a master plan for you: the optimal path to get you there. This preplanned route beautifully represents God's ultimate plan for your life. Remember, before you were born, God wrote His perfect will for you in a book, meticulously planning every single day.

Let me clarify that I am not teaching predestination in the sense that every decision is fixed, and we have no choice. Many Christians mistakenly believe this, often evident in casual conversations and prayers, leading to doctrines of *whatever will be, will be.* If this were true, rather than praying, we could just sit back and watch what happens. This common misunderstanding of God's sovereignty, which assumes everything that happens is the will of God, is so widespread it deserves its own book to fully address.

Wouldn't it be wonderful if God's will were as unmistakably obvious as the GPS, with the preplanned route highlighted on the screen? Instead of trying to figure it out, all we would have to do is look, listen, and follow the step-by-step directions.

But what happens if we accidentally make a wrong turn? The GPS immediately goes to work to help us get back on course. It might say, "If possible, make a U-turn," or "Recalculating." Even though the GPS has plotted the best route, we can override its instructions. The beauty of it is this: if we deviate from the chosen route, the GPS does not abandon the destination; it recalculates and adjusts our next steps to guide us back onto the best path.

All of this became clear in that sacred moment as I stood in the hotel room with those words alive in my spirit: "At this moment, you are in the center of My perfect will." Through my years of extensive travel, I have made more than my fair share of wrong turns. Sometimes getting back on track is quick and easy; other times, it's complicated and time-consuming. The overarching truth, however, is that no matter how many wrong turns we make, no matter how far we drift from the preplanned route, the GPS will never stop recalculating, constantly endeavoring to guide us back to the chosen path.

I sense a special presence of the Lord as I write this. When Paul and Barnabas got into strife and veered from God's perfect will for their partnership, God immediately began recalculating. It's even possible He had already foreseen their wrong turn and had a backup plan in place. Jesus explained to my friend that even though God, in His mercy, rewrote some pages in their books, both Paul and Barnabas faced additional challenges and hardships as a direct result of stepping out of God's original plan for their ministry assignment.

The key to my understanding hinged on these three words: "At this moment." With regard to what God had written in my book, I knew I had drifted, but the emphasis on those words brought clarity. If you make a wrong turn in your car, you are no longer on the best route to your destination. But the moment new instructions are given, and you follow them, you are instantly back on track. You might still be off the original path, but by following the recalculated directions of the GPS, you are, at that moment, in the center of its *perfect will.*

The day after receiving this revelation, I shared my experience with the people at my meeting. I told them, "You might be completely out of the will of God in the grand scheme of things. You may even be on the wrong continent. But if I was in the center of God's perfect will last night, I am persuaded that I am in the center of His perfect will as I stand here teaching, which means that, at this very moment, *you* are also in the center of His perfect will." I explained that some of them might have strayed far from God's overall plan, but by following His step-by-step instructions that led them to that meeting, they were now exactly where He wanted them to be. The GPS analogy provided a significant breakthrough for both me and everyone in the room that day.

The Path of the Righteous

As I continued to reflect on the GPS concept, another relevant Scripture came to mind:

> *But* ***the path of the righteous*** *is like the light of dawn, which shines brighter and brighter until full day.* **(Proverbs 4:18 ESV)**

As we have seen, a satellite navigation system plots a precalculated route, a path that is highlighted by the system. Building on Psalm 139:16, God has such a preordained route planned for each of us, a day-by-day blueprint leading to the fulfillment of His perfect will. We've established this is not a rigid predestination, for we can make wrong turns along the way, either by accident or by intentionally overriding God's instructions. Yet, just as our GPS relentlessly adjusts the route to help us stay on track, so too does God continually guide us back to His path.

Proverbs 4:18 uses the phrase "the path of the righteous." Could this "path" be synonymous with God's preordained plan we read about in Psalm 139? At this point, it seems good to include another verse that sheds more light on this truth:

> ***The steps of a good man are ordered by the LORD,*** *And He delights in his way. Though he fall, he shall not be utterly cast down; For the LORD upholds him with His hand.* **(Psalm 37:23-24 NKJV)**

We have looked at a handful of Scriptures that reveal the richness of God's language: a divine "book," a defined "path," "ordered steps," and a specific "way," all representing God's perfect will for each individual. It's important to note the latter part of Psalm 37:24: "Though he fall, he shall not be utterly cast down; For the LORD upholds him with His hand." This is deeply comforting. God has ordained steps for you, a distinct path, but you may stumble or even stray. Yet, the Lord does not change His mind about His ultimate plan. When you fall, He is there, ready to pick you up and help you get back on the path that represents His perfect will for your life.

Like the Light of Dawn

So, how can you know the perfect will of God? How can you be certain you're on the right path; the one God has so carefully mapped out for you? Let's revisit Proverbs 4:18:

> *But the path of the righteous is like the* ***light of dawn, which shines brighter and brighter*** *until full day.* **(Proverbs 4:18 ESV)**

This verse tells us that the path starts out in darkness. Prior to the light of dawn, the path cannot be seen. In that total darkness, you are unable to see how or where to take the first step. You may be eager to *do something*, but attempting to step forward then would be unwise, a move guided by guesswork and human reason. This is like driving off in your car before the GPS has finished loading the directions. You're moving, but you may not be going in the right direction. It's important to remember that getting in a hurry usually doesn't save time. Let me share a short but effective prayer that I pray often when the path seems dark:

> "Father, show me the next step."

Imagine yourself in this scenario: the sun hasn't risen, so you are in complete darkness. You're eager to get moving, but stepping forward blindly would be unwise. Human reason often dictates that if we aren't moving, we aren't progressing. But sometimes, the next step is to simply stand still. Here is a powerful truth: you do not have to be moving to be in the perfect will of God! This is confirmed by a well-known Scripture:

> *Be still, and know that I am God;* **(Psalm 46:10 NKJV)**

How many people do you know who are comfortable being still? And yet, many times, this is exactly what God desires. If I have asked God for wisdom and direction, and there is no light on my path, what harm does it do to stand still? To wait for the light of dawn? This light often manifests for me as a recurring thought, a persistent impression that lingers in my mind. If you are earnestly seeking the Lord for direction, these lingering thoughts may very well be your dawn breaking, beginning to light up your path.

Just remember, this initial light is not the noonday sun. If you wait for God to fully light up your entire path before taking any steps, you may never fulfill His will. God's Word teaches that our path begins in darkness, then comes dawn, enough light to take the first step. As we consistently take the steps God reveals, more light is likely to appear. The path then becomes brighter and clearer, until, before we know it, it shines with the brightness of the "full day."

We see a compelling example of this with Abraham:

> *Now the LORD had said to Abram: 'Get out of your country, From your family and from your father's house,* ***to a land that I will show you.*** **(Genesis 12:1 NKJV)**

> *By faith Abraham obeyed when he was called to go out to the place which he would receive as an inheritance. And* ***he went out, not knowing where he was going.*** **(Hebrews 11:8 NKJV)**

God told Abraham to get up and go, but at that moment, he didn't know *where* he was supposed to go. The path was dark. Should he go north, south, east, or west? How was he to choose his initial direction? All we know is that he was told to go with the assurance that, as he went, God would show him the destination. Based on the Scriptures we've examined, I believe that as Abraham stepped out in faith, his path became progressively brighter and clearer, just like the "light of dawn."

Chapter 7: Led by the Spirit, Anchored in the Word

As we've discussed "the path of the righteous," the next question is: How can we find this path? How can we be certain of God's perfect will for our lives, especially when it often reveals itself so subtly, like the light of dawn?

Some Christians mistakenly believe that figures like Abraham, those honored in *The Hall of Faith* (Hebrews chapter 11), possessed a unique connection or ability that allowed God to lead them supernaturally—a connection they believe is unavailable to us today. But the truth is exactly the opposite. As we discussed earlier regarding Elijah, the Old Testament prophets walked by faith, but they did not have the indwelling presence of the Holy Spirit like we do today. Let's look again at this foundational Scripture:

> *For as many as are led by the Spirit of God, they are the sons of God.* **(Romans 8:14 KJV)**

As we established earlier, being led by the Spirit of God is supernatural, but it is not always spectacular. Throughout my Christian journey, God has seldom led me in an overtly dramatic fashion. Instead, I have found that the Holy Spirit's leading usually manifests as a distinct thought, an inner knowing. One moment I have no idea what to do, and suddenly, the path becomes clear.

When a person is born again, they are "born of the Spirit of God" (John 3:6, 1 John 5:1). This means God's Spirit resides *within* the Christian believer—not externally, guiding through signs and circumstances, but internally. In fact, upon being born again, you and the Holy Spirit of God become one (1 Corinthians 6:17).

Therefore, for the children of God, seeking guidance through external signs, or that which is revealed to the five physical senses, is not Scriptural. Here is an important verse to remember:

> *For we walk by faith,* ***not by sight:*** **(2 Corinthians 5:7** KJV)

The following Scripture offers even greater insight into this inward leading:

> *The spirit of man is the candle of the LORD,* **(Proverbs 20:27 NKJV)**

So how does God bring light to your path? He leads you by His Spirit, and this verse clarifies *how*: His Spirit enlightens your spirit. Your spirit is His inner candle. If you seek to be led by external cues or by your intellect, you will likely veer off course, limiting yourself to human reason. Consider what Jesus Himself promised about the Holy Spirit's guidance:

> *However, when He, the Spirit of truth, has come,* ***He will guide you into ALL truth****; for He will not speak on His own authority, but whatever He hears He will speak; and He will tell you things to come.* **(John 16:13 NKJV)**

How much truth will the Holy Spirit lead you into? *All* of it! He will faithfully guide you into the fullness of God's perfect will for your life. And notice, Jesus also said the Holy Spirit "will tell you things to come," which includes revealing the very next step on the path God has ordained for you.

The Light of God's Word

To understand how the Holy Spirit leads us into all truth, we need to revisit this Scripture in which Jesus gives us a precise definition of truth:

> *Sanctify them by Your truth.* **Your word is truth. (John 17:17 NKJV)**

Jesus defined truth as the Word of God. If the Holy Spirit is leading us into all truth, and God's Word is that truth, then the Holy Spirit will often guide us through the written Word of God. Much of what we need to know about the perfect will of God is already written within the pages of the Holy Bible.

We have learned that the Holy Spirit communicates with us in our spirit. Sometimes He brings understanding by quickening something from the Word of God. The Holy Spirit cannot and will not lead us in a way that contradicts the written Word of God. They are always in perfect agreement with each other and with God the Father, as clearly revealed in this verse:

> *For there are three that bear witness in heaven:* ***the Father, the Word, and the Holy Spirit; and these three are one.*** **(1 John 5:7 NKJV)**

This is why one of the foremost ways the Holy Spirit guides us is by the Word of God. The following two verses provide more insight:

> *The entrance of Your words gives light;* **(Psalm 119:130 NKJV)**

> *Your word is a lamp to my feet and a light to my path.* **(Psalm 119:105 NKJV)**

God frequently shines more light on our path through the written Word of God. Scripture remains the primary and most reliable way God speaks to us today. You might perceive a leading from the Holy Spirit, but the most important question you must always ask is this: "Does this perceived leading align with the written Word of God?" If not, then it definitely is not a leading from the Holy Spirit. Of all the points I've made in this book, this single sentence may be the most important, capable of saving you from a world of unnecessary hurt and confusion. Let me repeat it: *If you believe you have a leading from the Holy Spirit, and that leading does not line up with the written Word of God, the leading is not of God.* There are absolutely no exceptions to this standard. The written Word of God is our anchor. No matter how strong a feeling, impression, or circumstance seems, we stay safe only when our lives and decisions remain steadfastly fixed to what God has already said.

This book is dedicated not just to understanding God's will, but to *praying out* His will. One of the most effective ways to pray out the will of God is to pray His Word. God's Word *is* His will.

I have a saying, "There is a time to *pray* and a time to *say*." Let me explain. After I have prayed a *prayer of faith*, I often turn that prayer into a *declaration of faith*. At this point, I'm not asking God for something again but rather declaring what He has already said about the matter in His Word. Here is an example based on Romans 8:14:

> "I am a son of God; I am led by the Spirit of God, and I always know what to do. Therefore, I know exactly what to do about..."

At the end of this declaration of faith, I add the specific situation for which I'm expecting guidance.

As you grow in the knowledge of God's Word, you will develop a more effective prayer life and an increasing awareness of the Holy Spirit's leadings.

Chapter 8: Is God in Control?

Let's return to a concept I touched on earlier: the notion of God's sovereignty, often misinterpreted as the belief that every circumstance, every event, and every outcome must be the will of God. I call this the "Whatever will be, will be" doctrine. These are the very people who seek God's will by asking Him to open and close doors, a method we've already shown to be unscriptural for New Testament believers. This approach neglects both the leading of the Holy Spirit and the guidance of the Word—the two primary ways God leads us today. One of the most common statements you'll hear from this camp is, "God is in control." Let's examine the truth of that statement.

Many years ago, I was invited to speak at a church where the pastor consistently taught the "God is in control" doctrine. It permeated nearly every message, and consequently, most of his congregation embraced this belief. I found it challenging to engage in even casual conversation without this doctrine surfacing.

As a Bible teacher, I prefer not to discuss Scripture outside the pulpit unless someone is genuinely seeking a deeper understanding. In my early ministry, I often fell into the trap of debating the Word, which usually left both parties frustrated and more entrenched in their original positions. I've since learned to redirect questions about the Bible to my books and videos, recognizing that those who really want to know the truth will take the time to refer to my materials. I have found that, more often than not, people aren't interested in truth if it demands change, because change is rarely comfortable.

Back to my story: I was in this church on a Wednesday night, and the title of my teaching was "Is God in Control?" I had prepared diligently, confident my teaching would offer a much-needed correction to the pervasive belief that God is in control *of everything*. This church had a tradition of lengthy, vibrant praise and worship sessions before the teaching. That night they sang a song I had never heard before and haven't heard since. No one in the room knew what I planned to teach that night, so imagine my astonishment when the praise team launched into this new song, repeating only the phrase, "God is in control." It was one of those moments you couldn't make up if you tried.

They sang the song with great enthusiasm for at least fifteen or twenty minutes. I stood there thinking, "No way! You've got to be kidding me!" Was this the Lord confirming my teaching topic, or was the devil trying to intimidate me in hopes I would change my message? In my early ministry years, I sometimes carried a Sermon A (my intended message) and a Sermon B (my backup, in case I lost my nerve). But those days were long past. That night, I was determined to teach "Is God in Control?" no matter what.

While the younger me may have struggled to find the courage to follow a song like that by teaching the exact opposite, the longer and louder they sang, the more determined I became to pile up the Scriptures refuting their flawed theology.

Let me clarify my position. The people in this church believed God is in control of *everything*—if you fall and break your ankle, if you're in an automobile accident, if someone breaks into your home and steals your valuables, it must be part of the mysterious will of God. Scripture gives us some insight into the ultimate plan God has in mind for His Kingdom, for humanity, and even for the devil, so I am certainly not teaching that God has *no* control. But God has granted mankind free will, and this is an enormous factor in determining the outcomes in our individual lives and in shaping much of what unfolds on Earth.

When the song finally ended, I stepped to the pulpit, eager to get into the Word of God. The crowd was still energized. I began by asking, "How many of you believe that God is in control?" Fervent shouts of "Amen" filled the room. "What is He in control of?" I asked. The predictable answer: "Everything!" Then came my first challenge: " So if God is in control of everything, He's in control of all your thoughts, right? Surely none of you had a bad thought today?" It was as if someone had burst the enthusiasm balloon. "If God is in control of everything," I continued, "He was in control of every word that came out of your mouth today, so I'm sure nobody in this room said a bad word." The room grew progressively quieter. "And if God is in control of everything, He was in control of all your actions today, so I know none of you married couples had an argument on the way to church tonight." Yes, I was being intentionally sarcastic and provocative to drive the point home, rather than easing into it. This isn't always the best approach, but that night, it seemed necessary. By then, I had everyone's undivided attention.

I proceeded to question how, if God is not in control of our thoughts, our words, and our actions, we can possibly believe that He is in control of all the outcomes in our lives. If you take nothing else from this book, please grasp this: your thoughts, your words, and your actions significantly shape the direction of your life. Yes, other factors exist, but these three are monumental. If you're dissatisfied with the results you're seeing in your life, I urge you to examine your thoughts, your words, and your actions.

I once heard a well-known minister refer to the idea of God being in control of everything as "No-Fault Religion." If you believe that every event in your life is part of God's perfect plan, it conveniently exempts you from personal responsibility. Whatever happens, it's not *your* fault. This way of thinking may be comforting, but it can seriously mislead believers about how God actually works in our lives. Why would we ever pray, "Father, Your will be done," if we truly believe God's will is going to happen no matter what?

Perhaps you are wondering how the congregation responded to my message that night. A Scripture describing some of the Apostle Paul's teaching sessions sums it up perfectly:

> *And some believed the things which were spoken, and some believed not.* **(Acts 28:24 KJV)**

As ministers of the Gospel, we are called by God to study to show ourselves approved and to yield to the leading of the Holy Spirit, offering our listeners the best possible opportunity to hear the truth. However, we are not responsible for making them believe. Even God Himself, by His own design, chooses not to compel everyone to believe the truth. The following Scripture makes this clear:

> *I exhort therefore, that, first of all, supplications, prayers, intercessions, and giving of thanks, be made for all men; For kings, and for all that are in authority; that we may lead a quiet and peaceable life in all godliness and honesty. For this is good and acceptable in the sight of God our Saviour;* ***Who will have all men to be saved, and to come unto the knowledge of the truth.*** **(1 Timothy 2:1-4 KJV)**

God's perfect will is that *all* people come to the knowledge of the truth and are saved. Yet, despite this being His will, not everyone who hears the truth believes.

That night, after my teaching, I heard some people in the parking lot mocking me and the idea that God is *not* in control of everything. In the days and weeks that followed, however, others approached me, sharing that this teaching answered many long-held questions and marked a significant turning point in their lives.

Chapter 9: Decisions Shape Your Destiny

Let's take a moment to review our framework. We've established that the perfect will of God for your life consists of three core components:

1. Receiving all that God has for you to receive
2. Becoming all that God desires for you to be
3. Accomplishing all that God has called you to do

We then learned that to effectively receive, become, and accomplish, we must position ourselves in the right places, with the right people, engaging in the right activities, at the right time. But how do we consistently arrive at the *right places*? I'm convinced that this process begins with *making right decisions.* I want to show you, from Scripture, why making right decisions is arguably the most important thing in your life:

> ***Wisdom is the principal thing;*** *Therefore get wisdom. And in all your getting, get understanding.* **(Proverbs 4:7 NKJV)**

Having examined this verse in dozens of translations, I found that most simply state that wisdom is *the most important thing*. So if anyone ever asks what the most important thing in your life is, you know exactly how to answer.

But what is wisdom? How can we define it? First, before answering that, we need to understand that the Bible draws a sharp distinction between human wisdom and the wisdom of God:

> *And my speech and my preaching was not with enticing words of* ***man's wisdom****, but in demonstration of the Spirit and of power: That your faith should not stand in* ***the wisdom of men****, but in the power of God. Howbeit we speak wisdom among them that are perfect: yet not* ***the wisdom of this world****, nor of the princes of this world, that come to nought: But we speak* ***the wisdom of God*** *in a mystery, even* ***the hidden wisdom, which God ordained*** *before the world unto our glory:* **(1 Corinthians 2:4-5 KJV)**

> *For* ***the wisdom of this world*** *is foolishness with God. For it is written, 'He catches the wise in their own craftiness';* **(1 Corinthians 3:19 NKJV)**

> *Oh, the depth of the riches both of* ***the wisdom and knowledge of God!*** **(Romans 11:33 NKJV)**

Given that the wisdom of man is deemed foolishness with God, Proverbs 4:7 cannot be referring to *human* wisdom as the most important thing. Here is my definition of the wisdom of God:

The Wisdom of God is the God-given ability to make right decisions.

Recall James 1:5, where we're instructed to pray for wisdom. If we insert our definition of the wisdom of God, it means that whenever we aren't sure what to do, we should ask God to show us the right decision. This is asking for His wisdom, and it is, without question, the most important thing in your life. Those who dismiss or misunderstand this truth are left relying solely on human wisdom, which God explicitly calls "foolishness." My interpretation of asking God for His wisdom is asking Him to show me the right decisions to make to fulfill His perfect will.

Before you can receive all, become all, and accomplish all, you must be in the right places, with the right people, doing the right activities, at the right time. This *divine positioning* begins with making right decisions. Although I am not aware of the author, the following statement is profound: "You make decisions, then your decisions make you." In other words, *your decisions shape your destiny*. A single right decision can lead to a life filled with good things, while one wrong decision can bring a lifetime of heartache and sorrow. Since wisdom is the most important thing in my life, I am absolutely convinced that the most important prayer I can pray is one asking God to show me the right decisions to make.

A Quality Decision: You're Halfway There

Once you make the right decision about something, you are halfway there. Halfway where? Halfway on your journey to the right places, where you will find the right people and engage in the right activities at the right time—so you can receive all that God has for you to receive, become all that God desires for you to be, and accomplish all that God has called you to do.

Years ago, I heard a minister use the phrase "quality decision." A brief internet search reveals that the average person makes about 35,000 decisions each day. While the exact number may be uncertain, the point is we are constantly making choices. Some decisions may be of little consequence, yet others are life-altering. While I'm not persuaded that God is concerned with every single decision we make each day, surely He has great interest in those related to the fulfillment of His perfect will. A *quality* decision, or what another minister friend, Pastor Jim Frease, calls a "defining decision," is one that has the potential to shape your destiny. Pastor Jim also talks about "pivotal points" and "monumental moments." Could it be that these *pivotal points* and *monumental moments* are a result of our *defining decisions*?

Let me illustrate what I mean by a quality decision and why it's only the starting point toward fulfilling the perfect will of God. I recall one January when I set a goal to reduce my body weight by at least fifty pounds over the course of the coming year. Throughout my adult life, I had made many decisions that I needed to lose weight, but this time was different. What made this one a *quality* decision? I not only made the decision, but I immediately formulated a step-by-step strategy to support it. A true quality decision will be accompanied by a plan of action. Right decisions must be followed by right steps to bring you to the right places, people, activities, and timing. Before I could get rid of fifty pounds, I had to be serious enough not only to make the decision but also to combine action with that decision. There were specific things I had to do, and things I had to refuse to do every day. The good news is that by making a quality decision and following a specific plan, I achieved my goal, shedding just over fifty pounds that year. One of my favorite adages seems fitting here: "Failing to plan is planning to fail." This leads to another simple prayer I pray on a regular basis:

> "Father, show me the right decisions to make and the right steps to take."

In my personal weight-reduction example, I prayed about the specific steps to take, and I saw all of them ahead of time. This is usually not the case. As I've mentioned, many times the Lord will only reveal step one. Every fiber of your being will want to know the second step before taking the first, but often, you'll only discover what comes next after you have moved forward. Take the first step in the direction that seems right and watch as your path grows brighter.

Here's another personal example of taking corresponding steps of action after making a major decision. My wife and

I were content living in our hometown of Poplar Bluff, Missouri. We had no intention of ever leaving. One day, we decided to take a weekend trip to Branson, Missouri—a place we had visited many times over the years. Since looking at houses is one of our favorite hobbies, we decided to drive through some residential neighborhoods just for fun. Moving to Branson was not on our radar.

This particular trip did not go well. We had found a few houses online we wanted to drive by, but we struggled to locate them and ended up off the beaten path, seemingly in the middle of nowhere. We returned home frustrated.

Remember earlier when I talked about recurring, lingering thoughts? Well, early the following week, this thought began to surface: we needed to go back to Branson the next weekend. It made no sense, but the urge wouldn't leave me. When I mentioned it to my wife, she was not in favor at all. I tried to put the idea on hold, but it persisted until finally I said, "We're going." We had no clear reason, perhaps just to redeem the lackluster trip from the week before.

The second trip was better. This time we actually managed to find the houses we had picked out. Remember, we weren't looking with the intention of moving, just for pure enjoyment. Early the following week, the exact same thing happened again: I felt a strong prompting to return to Branson for a third consecutive weekend. When I mentioned this to my wife, she said, "No way!" I agreed with her; it sounded crazy. Yet the thought of returning grew even stronger, until finally we agreed, "We have to go back."

So, we did. This time, we decided to contact a realtor and go inside some of the houses we had driven by. It still didn't make sense because we had no desire to relocate. During the process of booking a condo for the weekend, I noticed some other condos for sale. That caught my attention. A thought struck me: perhaps it would be a good idea to buy a condo as a nightly rental investment property, which we could also occasionally use ourselves.

Long story short: eight weeks later, we owned a condo *and* were living in a 5,000-square-foot dream home in Branson, Missouri. Within a few short weeks of these purchases, both properties had nearly doubled in value. My realtor remarked, "Rich, you got the last good deal in Branson." Prices continued to boom. We leased the condo to a tenant for three years, then sold it for double our purchase price, and we still live in our home at the time of this writing. This entire journey, from a *foolish* lingering thought to miraculous provision, is a testimony of following God's leading, even when it defied human reason.

Before making this geographic move, the Lord had been dealing with me about entering the television ministry. Once we got to the right place, Branson, I met the right people who helped me do just that. I'm not sure this could have happened while living in Poplar Bluff because the people with the expertise in this field weren't there.

Appearance, Need, and Pressure from Others

At the time of this writing, there is a challenging situation happening within our family. Family members have various ideas as to what might be the best decisions and steps to resolve the issue. In seeking the Lord, I have not received any clear direction, so I have not given a lot of input.

Now, I sense pressure mounting from others trying to persuade me to take certain steps. These suggestions are based on the appearance and the obvious needs, not the leading of the Holy Spirit. I am determined not to make any decisions in this matter based on appearance, need, or pressure from others. Until God's wisdom lights my path, I will simply stand still.

Chapter 10: Putting It All Together—Your One-Minute Daily Prayer

Early in this book, I mentioned one of my teachings called "My One-Minute Daily Prayer," which served as the inspiration and foundation for these pages. I've received a number of testimonies from individuals whose lives have been transformed by the simple prayer I'm about to share. My earnest hope is that you will experience the same.

This prayer takes less than a minute to pray, but the length isn't the focus. Its true value lies in providing a starting point for praying out the perfect will of God. Remember, it's not about *how long* a prayer is, but *how effective* it is.

Here is an important question to ask regarding any prayer: "Is this a prayer that God can answer?" This might rub some Christians the wrong way because many believe that God can answer any prayer. Not so. God cannot answer a prayer asking Him to do something He has *already* done, or something He has commanded *us* to do. For example, let's say you have a nephew you call Little Johnnie, and he is not yet a Christian. Your prayer for him may resemble this: "Lord, save Little Johnnie." Let's examine this prayer for its effectiveness. We have already seen in Scripture that God wants Little Johnnie to be saved and that the provision for his salvation has already been made. Therefore, praying "Lord, save him" is essentially asking God to do what He has already done. Furthermore, it is asking Him to do the very thing He has commanded us to do: proclaim the Gospel. The following Scripture reveals exactly what must happen for Little Johnnie to be saved:

> *How then shall they* **call** *on Him in whom they have not* **believed**? *And how shall they* **believe** *in Him of whom they have not* **heard**? *And how shall they* **hear** *without a* **preacher**? *And how shall they preach unless they are sent?* **(Romans 10: 14-15 NKJV)**

For Little Johnnie to be saved, he must *hear* the gospel, *believe*, and *call* upon the Lord. And before he can do any of this, *someone* must present the gospel to him. Even though this verse uses the word "preacher," in this case the preacher is simply the one who communicates the gospel message. Notice what Jesus said about prayer as it relates to the specific subject we are reviewing:

> *Then He said to them, "The harvest truly is great, but the laborers are few; therefore* **pray the Lord of the harvest to send out laborers** *into His harvest."* **(Luke 10:2 NKJV)**

So, rather than just praying, "Lord, save Little Johnnie," a more effective prayer would be:

> "Father, I ask You send laborers across Little Johnnie's path to present the gospel to him so he can hear, believe and be saved."

Do you see the notable difference in these two prayers? We are still talking about praying out the will of God but more specifically, how to do so effectively.

We have seen that God's perfect will does not automatically come to pass, but rather usually requires our cooperation. If His will were automatic, prayer would lose much of its purpose in our lives. Instead, prayer serves as a vital tool to both discover and walk out the perfect will of God. This *one-minute daily prayer* systematically incorporates the core components of the perfect will of God that we've already explored.

Let's revisit these now:

1. Receiving all that God has for you to receive
2. Becoming all that God desires for you to be
3. Accomplishing all that God has called you to do

But before we can begin receiving, becoming, and accomplishing, we must be in the right places, with the right people, engaging in the right activities, at the right time. And this process begins with making the right decisions and taking the right steps. This isn't complicated, but it requires intentional, Spirit-led engagement.

Now, it's time to bring everything together into one concise yet complete prayer. I'm not suggesting this is the *only* prayer you should pray each day, but it's a great starting point. Here is the prayer that this entire book has been building toward:

> "Father, today I ask You to show me the right decisions to make and the right steps to take to lead me to the right places, the right people, the right activities, at the right time, so I can receive all that You have for me to receive, so I can become all that You desire for me to be, so I can accomplish all that You have called me to do, so I can fulfill Your perfect will that was recorded in my book before I was even born."

Now *that* is an effective prayer!

We could just pray the shorter version we examined earlier—asking the Father to fill us with the knowledge of His will in all wisdom and spiritual understanding—but I find that this expanded prayer provides a much richer understanding. One of the great benefits of prayer, especially when we are praying according to the Word of God, is the privilege of hearing ourselves speak these truths. We're not adding extra words to impress or persuade God, but when we hear ourselves pray out the details of God's perfect will, it enhances our understanding. Merely saying, "Father, Your will be done," is general, vague, and often requires little thought or personal engagement. Adding the specifics of what God's will actually entails, as outlined in the prayer above, brings clarity to exactly what we are expecting to receive.

Would you be willing to make a quality decision right now to pray this prayer at least once every day for the next thirty days? If you take this step, I believe you will be astounded by how much brighter and clearer your path becomes. I eagerly look forward to hearing your testimony of the life-changing impact of this *one-minute daily prayer.*

Chapter 11: Praying in the Spirit

One of my most valuable prayer practices for praying out the perfect will of God, is *praying in the Spirit.* This, as we will explore through several Scriptures, refers to *praying in other tongues.*

Since there are many varied beliefs and even outright objections to speaking in tongues, it would be easy to sidestep this topic. Some teach that speaking in tongues passed away centuries ago; others claim it's from the devil; and still others acknowledge its existence but believe it's only for select believers. However, an understanding of this subject is important if you want your prayer life to reach its full potential.

While this book won't provide a complete teaching on being filled with the Holy Spirit and speaking in tongues, I want to address those who have already had this experience. My focus is to take a closer look at what speaking in tongues truly is: a supernatural form of prayer. Simply put, speaking in tongues is praying in tongues, which is praying in the Spirit. Let's examine the Scriptures:

For he who speaks in a tongue ***does not speak to men but to God,*** *for no one understands him; however, in the spirit he speaks mysteries.* **(1 Corinthians 14:2 NKJV)**

Several key insights are revealed in this single verse. First, when you speak in tongues, you are speaking directly to God. What do we call speaking to God? Prayer. Thus, speaking in tongues is more accurately described as *praying in tongues.* Second, no human understands what is being said. This dispels the misconception that tongues refers to human languages. As we will see in the next few verses, speaking any known human language engages the mind, while praying in tongues transcends intellectual understanding. Third, speaking (or praying) in tongues is called speaking "in the spirit," which is more accurately called *praying* in the spirit.

The following verse gives more insight:

For if I pray in a tongue, ***my spirit prays,*** *but* ***my understanding is unfruitful.*** **(1 Corinthians 14:14 NKJV)**

Again, we see that speaking in tongues is more accurately termed praying in tongues. Other Scriptures confirm that man is comprised of spirit, soul, and body (1 Thessalonians 5:23, Hebrews 4:12). Paul clearly states that when he prays in tongues, his spirit prays but his intellect is not engaged—he doesn't understand what he's saying with his natural mind. However, this "unfruitful" understanding isn't a weakness—it's actually a divine design that allows our spirit to pray beyond our natural limitations. Instead of our mind directing the prayer, it is our spirit praying, reaching beyond the realm of human understanding. This supernatural bypass of our natural understanding enables our spirit to pray in perfect harmony with God's will.

Why, then, would you choose to pray in a language you don't understand? This question is directly addressed in the very next verse:

> *What is the conclusion then?* ***I will pray with the spirit****, and* ***I will also pray with the understanding****. I will sing with the spirit, and I will also sing with the understanding.* **(1 Corinthians 14:15 NKJV)**

Paul told us the decision he had come to in his prayer life: he would pray with his spirit (praying in tongues, which he didn't understand), and he would also pray with his understanding (praying in his known human language). It's interesting to me that Paul uses the words "I will" when referring to praying and singing in tongues just as with praying and singing in his known language. This signifies that we don't have to wait for the Holy Spirit to move upon us in a special way to speak in tongues, but rather that speaking in tongues is *an act of the will.*

Paul continues teaching about praying in tongues in the following verses:

> *Otherwise, if you* **bless with the spirit***, how will he who occupies the place of the uninformed say "Amen" at your*

> ***giving of thanks****, since he does not understand what you say? For* ***you indeed give thanks well****, but the other is not edified.* **(1 Corinthians 14:16-17 NKJV)**

We see three key phrases directly from Scripture: "pray with the spirit," "sing with the spirit," and now "bless with the spirit." But what does it mean to "bless with the spirit"? The verse itself gives us the answer: it is "giving of thanks."

We know Paul is referring to giving thanks in tongues here because he explicitly states that the listener "does not understand what you say." If the words were a known language, the listener would understand. The mention of "Amen" is also key. Since "Amen" is a response to prayer, we know that *blessing with the spirit* is specifically a prayer of thanksgiving.

Furthermore, Paul highlights the quality of this prayer: he states that "you indeed give thanks well." While praying in our known language, we are limited by our own understanding and may fall short of expressing the full depth of our gratitude. However, when we give thanks in tongues, we can have complete confidence that our words are adequate; God Himself declares that we are giving thanks well.

Paul reinforces this truth about our limitations in his letter to the Romans, stating plainly that we don't always know how to pray "as we ought." But he doesn't leave us there; he points us to the solution. Remember that the focus of this book is *praying out* the perfect will of God. The following verses demonstrate the vital connection between praying in the Spirit and the will of God perhaps better than any:

> ***Likewise the Spirit also helps in our weaknesses. For we do not know what we should pray for as we ought,*** *but the Spirit Himself makes intercession for us with groanings which cannot be uttered. Now He who searches the hearts knows what the mind of the Spirit is, because* ***He makes intercession for the saints according to the will of God.*** **(Romans 8:26-27 NKJV)**

Here is yet another reason why praying in tongues is so important:

> *He who speaks in a tongue* ***edifies himself,*** **(1 Corinthians 14:4 NKJV)**

Other translations of 1 Corinthians 14:4 use the following words and phrases: *improves himself, builds himself up, helps himself, is strengthened.*

The following verse confirms this truth:

> *But you, beloved,* ***building yourselves up*** *on your most holy faith,* ***praying in the Holy Spirit,*** **(Jude 1: 20 NKJV)**

If God has given us a supernatural means of *improving ourselves*, *building ourselves up*, *helping ourselves*, and *strengthening ourselves* by praying in tongues, how foolish would we be to ignore or reject it?

Considering the significant attention the Holy Spirit devotes to the subject of praying in tongues through the writings of Paul, it is difficult to comprehend how anyone could disregard its importance for us today.

I once had a neighbor who said, "Yes, I believe speaking in tongues still exists, it's just not for me." I was stunned by this statement. There was so much I wanted to say, but I refrained, knowing there was no room for discussion. I left that conversation wondering what God the Father must think of such a response. He gives a precious gift, extensively details its purpose and practice in the New Testament, only to have His own children declare "it's just not for me." Sadly, such an attitude often stems from a general lack of interest in spiritual things.

Let's recap the key takeaways from this chapter:

1. Speaking in tongues is speaking to God, which is prayer; therefore, speaking in tongues is more accurately called *praying in tongues.* (1 Corinthians 14:2)
2. *Tongues* refers to a supernatural language, not human languages. (1 Corinthians 14:2)
3. Praying in tongues is called *praying in the Spirit.* (1 Corinthians 14:2)
4. When praying in tongues, it is our spirit praying; our mind is not engaged. (1 Corinthians 14:14)

5. Praying in tongues is an act of the will, just as praying in a known language is. (1 Corinthians 14:15)
6. In addition to "praying with the spirit" and "singing with the spirit," we can "bless with the spirit," which is giving thanks to God in tongues. (1 Corinthians 14:16-17)
7. When we "bless with the spirit," we are giving thanks well. (1 Corinthians 14:16-17)
8. Praying in tongues is helpful when we don't know what or how to pray. (Romans 8:26-27)
9. When we pray in tongues, we are praying according to the will of God. (Romans 8:26-27)
10. Praying in tongues is a means of personal edification. (1 Corinthians 14:4, Jude 1:20)

With these truths in mind, I encourage you to make praying in tongues a daily priority. As you do, you will find yourself walking more fully in God's perfect will.

Chapter 12: Closing Thoughts and Encouragement

As we come to the close of this book, I want to leave you with a very simple but powerful truth: you *do not* have to figure out a plan for your life. Before you ever took your first breath, God wrote a book about you, recording *His* perfect will for every single day. His desire is not to hide that plan from you, but to lead you into the fullness of it every step of the way.

You now have several keys to help you cooperate with God's great plan:

- A clear, biblical picture of what His perfect will looks like—receiving all He has for you, becoming all He desires you to be, and accomplishing all He has called you to do
- A simple, Scriptural way to ask for wisdom and direction: "Father, show me what to do," and "Father, show me the next step."
- A practical daily prayer that brings together right decisions, right steps, right places, right people, right activities, and right timing

- For those who have received it, the ability to pray in the Spirit—praying beyond your understanding, in perfect harmony with the will of God

None of this is complicated, but if it's new to you, implementing what you've learned will take some time and intentional effort.

We have learned that God's will is not an unsolvable mystery. His Word says He wants us to be filled with the knowledge of His will in all wisdom and spiritual understanding. We have also seen that God will give wisdom to those who ask in faith. He orders our steps, lights our path, and even *recalculates* when we take a wrong turn.

If there are blank pages in your book, or seasons where you know you've missed it, remember this: God has not thrown the book away. He is for you, not against you. He is still writing, still leading, and still willing to direct your steps from this moment forward. Condemnation looks back and paralyzes. Faith looks forward and looks up, asking, "Father, what do You want me to do now?"

If you pray in tongues, I encourage you to do so alongside your one-minute daily prayer. Pray the prayer with your understanding, and then spend time praying in the Spirit. As you do, you can be sure of this: your spirit is praying perfectly, according to the will of God, about your decisions, your steps, your relationships, your assignments, and your future.

As with most teaching sessions, when it comes time to close, I'm aware there is so much more that could be said on this subject. The will of God, and how to pray it out, is far too rich to be exhausted in a single book. My goal has not been to say everything that could be said, but to give you a solid foundation to begin walking in these truths for yourself. As you do, the Holy Spirit will continue to teach you, lead you, and unfold more of God's perfect will day by day. With that in mind, here is my prayer for you:

> "Father, I ask You to give this reader a clear understanding of these precious truths. Help them receive all that You have for them to receive, become all that You desire for them to be, and accomplish all that You have called them to do. Lead them into the center of Your perfect will for every day that remains in their book. In Jesus' Name, amen."

Here is my recommendation to you:

- Set aside a space of uninterrupted time every day for the next thirty days.
- Pray the one-minute daily prayer.
- If you can, add time praying in the Spirit.
- Then watch—expectantly—for the wisdom, nudges, corrections, and opportunities that begin to come.

I fully expect that as you do this, you will begin to see patterns of divine timing, protection, provision, and connection that you may recognize only in hindsight as the hand of God. When this happens, give Him the glory. It was His will. It was His wisdom. It was His Spirit. But it was your choice to ask, to believe, and to follow.

Now you can go forward with confidence and begin praying out the perfect will of God for your life. My encouragement to you is simple:

- Don't wait until you feel *spiritual enough* to start.
- Don't wait hoping to see the entire path before making a move.
- Start where you are.
- Pray what you know.
- As light comes, take the next step.

If you will pray the one-minute daily prayer you've learned, and take the steps God shows you, your life will begin to transform. Your awareness of His leading will grow. Your confidence in His will for you will deepen. Your decisions will increasingly line up with *His* wisdom instead of *your own* reasoning. And one day you'll look back and realize that your path—which began as just the faint light of dawn—has truly grown brighter and brighter and is now approaching the noonday sun.

About The Author

Rich Stocks is an Author, Bible Teacher, Business Owner, and Certified Holistic Health Coach. Born in Poplar Bluff, Missouri, he grew up in a Christian home. At the age of 19, Rich heard the Word of Faith message for the first time, igniting a deep hunger to know more about God and walking by faith. He began reading and listening to teaching materials in every spare moment he could find. During this season, he also received the baptism with the Holy Spirit and spoke with other tongues. Just a few weeks later, Rich was invited to speak at a small church. Since then, the Lord has opened doors for him to teach the Word of God on radio and television, as well as to business groups, Bible schools, and churches across the United States, Mexico, Australia, New Zealand, Papua New Guinea, and the Philippines. He currently hosts *The Healthy Christian*, a television broadcast airing throughout the United States and Africa.

Rich has had a strong passion for health, healing, and longevity since early childhood. In addition to teaching on these topics from a Scriptural perspective, he entered the wellness industry in 1997. Through both his teaching and his health coaching, he has helped tens of thousands of people apply Biblical principles and practical strategies for spiritual, physical, and financial well being.

Although he embraced the message of prosperity found in the Bible, Rich's early years were marked by financial struggles. When presented with the opportunity to start his business for just six dollars, he was so broke that it took him several days to come up with the money to get started. As the Lord helped him learn and apply the Biblical principles of success, what started very small quickly expanded nationally and internationally. This growth provided Rich with the time and resources to attend and graduate from Rhema Bible College. He later returned to college (Central Methodist University) to complete a Bachelor of Science in Psychology, a degree he first began working on while still in high school.

Rich and his family had the privilege of living in Australia for a year in 2003, a season they greatly enjoyed. Today, Rich Stocks Ministries is based in Branson, Missouri.

Connect With Rich Stocks

Websites

Bible Teaching and Ministry – **RichStocks.org**

Free Health Evaluations and Supplements – **MineralDoctor.com**

Wellness Products and Services – **HealthyChristian.com**

YouTube Channel – **@RichStocksTheHealthyChristian**

Other Books by Rich Stocks

7 Reasons Why God Wants You To Have Money

Discover the divine purpose behind material wealth. In this book, Rich provides a strong foundation for Biblical prosperity. Once you understand exactly *why* God wants you to have money, your faith will be empowered to receive all that He desires for you.

Simple3Slim – *Three Simple Steps That Will Transform Your Body And Your Life*

Simple3Slim is one of the simplest, most effective weight management guides you will ever find. Now you can take the weight off and keep it off for good by creating a lifelong eating plan designed specifically for you.

The Secret Of An Unshakable Life

We are living in perilous times, but God expects every believer to walk in continuous peace. In this book, Rich provides real, Biblical answers for overcoming life's five major kinds of trouble, empowering you to live an unshakable life even when the world around you is in chaos.

www.ingramcontent.com/pod-product-compliance
Lightning Source LLC
LaVergne TN
LVHW010628100826
845148LV00014B/3158

* 9 7 9 8 9 8 5 1 1 4 3 1 7 *